Big Message,
Short Story

Big Message, Short Story

Chris Hollyfield

ISBN: 1542752108
ISBN 13: 9781542752107

Table of Contents

My name is Chris Hollyfield. I was born with dwarfism, a condition that prevents people from growing taller than four feet nine inches. I stand only four foot four. I did not let this, or other obstacles, stand in my way, nor keep me from doing what I wanted and loved. With a positive attitude, I have overcome challenges, lived out my dreams, and changed lives. I have endured teasing, bullying, and skepticism. Through all the tough times, I never gave up. I kept a "can do" attitude, which allowed me to reach my childhood goals and dreams. I have been on several national television shows, including the World Wrestling Entertainment star known as Little Boogeyman. The television experience helped build the platform for the "Got Respect Tour", which involved traveling to schools across the country to make a difference in the fight against bullying.

"I'm different to MAKE a difference." Chris Hollyfield

PART 1

Who is Chris Hollyfield?

_⟋⟍_

IT WAS 1967. ARETHA FRANKLIN'S smash hit "Respect" had been released. The song was music to my parent's ears. They were starting to plan a family, and they were young and in love. My dad was an Airman First Class in the United States Air Force when my mom found out she was pregnant. On July 5, 1967, at 1:30 pm, Chris Hollyfield was born—weighing three pounds six ounces—at the Naval Hospital in Pensacola, Florida. The doctor had some unexpected news to tell my parents: their son was born with dwarfism. They didn't know what that meant, or what to expect, as they were both average height. Later, my siblings were born of average height. For the next ten years, my parents would have to travel to special doctors to monitor my growth. My legs were shaped different than other kids my age. The doctors called it bowlegs, which over the long haul would lead to severe pain in my knees and hips. It was also possible that any wrong activities, such as contact sports, could put me in a wheelchair for the rest of my life. So, as I got older, my mom had lots of concerns, because she would see my personality develop around a certain attitude: whatever big kids could do, so could I.

Watch out world, Chris Hollyfield is here!!

Me, at nine months old.

PART 2

Standing Tall

AT SIX YEARS OLD, I was dropped off by my mother for my first day of public school. Up until then, I had been in a relatively safe neighborhood with my own friends. I was never treated, or thought of, as being different. Public school was a whole new world.

Immediately, I ran into trouble. A couple of the older boys thought they should set themselves apart from the others right away by pointing out any differences in any of the other children. I was, of course, first on the list. The boys told me, in no uncertain terms, that I was "too short", and that I "didn't belong there". These were words I had not heard before, and now I had to deal with the emotional and mental backlash that came along with something so negative and new. These kids were honest-to-goodness bullies, and this turned out to be just one, in a string of defining moments, that would lead me to my chosen path later in life.

Feeling lost and alone, and not knowing what to do, I did what any six-year-old would do in the face of public rejection and humiliation—I cried. As the tears began to well up in my eyes, I fought hard against them. I fought them because I instinctively knew that once the first tear rolled down my cheek, the laughter from the crowd would get worse. Quickly scanning the growing crowd of children circled around me, I hoped to find a familiar face from the neighborhood to latch onto for support, or possibly even defense. I looked and looked but, couldn't find even one of my neighborhood friends. Even if I had found a friendly face, would it have made a difference? It would have been too late anyway, because the tears had started to fall freely, and the meaner kids were taking notice.

"Cry baby, cry baby—look at the short cry baby," they said, taunting me.

It was all too much for me to bear, and I turned and ran as far from the crowd as I could. I sat down against the red brick wall of the elementary school to hide my face and wept in private. It was only the first day of school, and it had already been a horrible experience. Would the rest of the year, or my school career in general, be like this?

For the next few days, I was verbally assaulted by the same kids in much the same way, until one day I had a brilliant idea. Next time, I thought, when they laughed and pointed, I would just ignore it all and keep walking.

At six years old, I was already stumbling upon a lesson I would eventually share with thousands of kids across the country: perception is reality. I decided that if I didn't give the meaner kids a target, they couldn't attack me.

The next day, I put my theory to the test. This time, when they called me short, I simply said, "Thanks for noticing," and continued on my way. Flabbergasted, the bigger kids were left speechless, and I had just learned an important lesson:

The power of a bully is only as strong as you let it be.

From then on out, I was able to fly under the radar and avoid confrontations. It was clear to nearly everyone that I was more than just my size, and no one to be messed with.

PART 3

Football Dreams

~~~⌒~~~

IT WAS THE SUMMER OF 1976, the year of the bicenten-
nial. I was turning nine years old and dreaming of playing professional football like my uncle—Willie Rogers,
number thirty-four, running back for the Houston Oilers,
before Hall of Famer Earl Campbell took over the
position.

My favorite football player in the '70s was my Uncle
Willie. He played for the Houston Oilers with
Coach Bum Phillips.

One day, my friends and I took our father's white
T-shirts to make homemade football jerseys. We wanted
to be like players on America's favorite team, the Dallas

6

Cowboys. (The Dallas Cowboys cheerleaders were also the most popular of the NFL cheerleaders in this era, and being typical boys, we started to notice that). I, being the ringleader of a group that included my three friends Johnny Smith, Derrick Taylor, and Boyd Wolf, would have them meet at my house to start crafting with black magic markers our own Dallas jerseys with our favorite player's numbers. Since I was the shortest of the crew, I picked, as my favorite player, Robert Newhouse, a full-back built like a brick house. Newhouse was small and stocky compared to most players. He had a low center of gravity and was very hard to bring down. I related to Newhouse, so I proudly sported the number forty-four on my dad's brand new white T-shirt, a shirt I had taken without asking. When my dad found out I had taken his new white T-shirt, he wasn't happy.

What that incident did was show my father the drive I had to continue pursuing my dreams. I wasn't handi-capped. I had a different perspective in this oversized world as an undersized young man. The bad news was my mom wouldn't let me sign up for football, feeling my size could cause me to have very serious injuries. The doctors didn't recommend that I play such a rough sport. For weeks, I begged to play because I loved the game, and it didn't sit well with me that I was being left out. I would still attend my friends' practices to support them. Not long after, the coaches asked me if I would like to be the team manager/hype guy to keep the players fired up. Of course, I said yes, I might not be playing, but I would be doing something more than just sitting and watching. That evening, I told my mom that I was part of the football team.

Once I explained what I would be doing, my everloving and supportive mother smiled and said, "That's the perfect role for you."

My dad came home one summer evening to give his family unexpected news. He told us he was to be stationed on a military base in Spangdahlem, Germany. My mom initially struggled with the news. We were very surprised that we were about to move over five thousand miles from friends and family.

I yelled with joy. "Dad, does this mean we are going on a plane?" I asked.

"Yes," replied my dad.

So that night we all sat around asking a million questions about the food, language, weather, and a hundred other things.

"I will get all the information from my boss in the next few days, to answer all your questions," said my dad.

My sister and I were so excited that we looked up Germany in the encyclopedia, curious about what our lives were going to be like outside the United States. As the summer went by, we started visiting our relatives throughout the United States. We knew our journey to Germany would limit our communication with them for the next three years to only telephone calls and letter writing.

In September 1978, the day had come for my dad to leave Little Rock AFB, and go to his next military base, Spangdahlem Air Base, to find housing for his family. Three months went by, and finally we got the call. It was midnight and we- my baby brother, sister, and I—were all sleeping in mom's bed. My dad called to tell my mom he had found housing, and we would be joining him in three weeks. I started jumping on the bed, excited to be with my dad and getting on that airplane. I had never been on an airplane before. I could barely contain my excitement! My mom became Wonder Woman for the next three weeks, getting our school records, winter clothes, shopping, packing, and setting up for the movers to ship our things. The worst thing about all this wasn't the fact I was leaving my friends, it was the vaccines and shots we had to get from the doctors before we could move to Germany. The shots hurt so bad I cried for days. My arms were swollen for a week.

The three weeks went by quickly. The clock struck 8 am. We were headed to the airport to have a jet take us to another country, so we could start our lives anew. We boarded the plane with three days of traveling ahead of us. The journey would take us from Little Rock, Arkansas, to Charleston, South Carolina, to Frankfurt, Germany. Poor mom wasn't sure what to expect with three young children, ages eleven, nine, and eight months, on a full flight, eight hours nonstop, and no playground for kids to entertain themselves. We were on a 747-jumbo jet watching *Grease*. As the flight went on, my sister and I, along with other children, started to get restless. The pilot came over the intercom system letting us know we were thirty minutes away from landing. We were asked to remain in our seats with our seat belts on. The plane was touching down when it hit some black ice. Our plane slid off the runway! Approaching the plane were fire rescue vehicles and police cars. Babies were crying, people were screaming. It was chaos. I haven't forgotten my first airplane experience.

When I was thirteen, I was finally allowed to participate in organized football. By then, the other kids my age were above my height, and my parents were leery about letting me on the field with kids bigger than me. My parents sat down with the head of the city league to discuss options while I waited nervously at home for good news. When my parents arrived home, I met them in the driveway, not wanting to wait for them to even get out of the car. They told me I could play, but on one condition: I would have to join the younger boys in the nine to eleven- year-old division. I was a little taken aback, but I quickly realized it didn't matter.

I was going to be able to play.

PART 4

Never Give Up

I WAS TURNING FOURTEEN, AND was very eager to start earning my own money, in addition to the small allowance I was getting every week, which was roughly five dollars. From a young age, I had always had it in my mind that I wanted to be" *the boss*", and be able to express my ideas. The reality was that I needed to work hard to one day get to that point. I asked my parents if I could get a job. They were supportive of it.

"Sure, if someone will give you a few hours to work for them, its fine with us," they said," but school comes first, then the job."

I went out one Saturday morning on my bike to search for that job. "Show me the money!" I had no clue where to go and what to say, so I stopped at different stores, and would ask the managers, "Could I work for you? I want to make some money, and I will show up every day. Just give me a chance."

I was driven to keep riding my bike all over town until someone said "yes." It started to get dark, and I had yet to find someone who had given me the answer I was looking for. I headed home with a lot of "no's," but I was not willing to give up. When I got home that night, I asked my dad, "Why don't people want to hire me?"

What I was about to hear wasn't something I was prepared for.

"Chris, things are going to be very rough for you, but no matter what, your mom and I love you with all our heart."

I was sitting there asking myself where my dad was going with this.

"Son, being that you are of short stature and won't grow to be much taller, a lot of places are going to turn you down for many different reasons," he said.

That was a blow to my ego. This had me thinking about how difficult it would be to be short all my life, and not given a fair chance.

My father embraced me. "Don't give up. Something good will happen."

I kept at it all right, to the point I would almost mock the managers. Weeks went by, and I saw Dino's Pizza in Satellite Beach was opening soon. I figured I would jump on the opportunity and be the first person asking for a job. At the tender age of fourteen, I had no experience whatsoever, but the manager asked me if I would take the job of passing out flyers. I immediately said yes before I even knew what the duties or pay were, because I was eager to just start working! We walked over to a table and sat down to eat some pizza while he told me about what I would be doing, and all the money I would be making... Wait for it...

"Chris," he said. "I will give you four dollars a day, a pitcher of soda, and a large pepperoni pizza."

All I could say was, "When do I start?" I had a huge Kool-Aid smile on my face.

I went home to tell my parents I got a job. They asked me about what I would be doing. I explained to them the details, and they said to make sure I did a good job. That night I started writing down what I was going to do with the four dollars a day that I was about to earn. That was twenty dollars for the week, unlike my friends, who got hired at McDonald's, and made about three thirty-five per hour. It was a big difference between what I would be making and what they would be making. This was my first job, and I was going to make the best of it.

I arrived early, around nine in the morning, to pick up the flyers to pass out all over the neighborhood until noon, which was the time I came back to get my *free* pizza and soda. Afterward, I would make one more round passing out flyers until about two in the afternoon. I would go back, get paid, and start again the next day. For a few weeks, I kept up the same routine. One day, while riding my bike through my neighborhood, two boys stopped me, curious about what I was doing.

"What are you up to?" they asked.

"I have a job, and I'm in charge of passing out the flyers for the pizza place."

"What do you get for doing it?"

"I get free pizza and soda."

"Can we help?"

"Sure."

What kid doesn't like pizza and soda? They were already interested, but I did not mention the extra four dollars I would receive. It would not be ideal to split that little bit of money between three people. The next day came, and I explained the routine to them—how we would pass out the flyers, and at noon we would go eat. They were up for it. I took them up to Dino's to eat at noon and introduced them to the manager as my buddies. I kept it short.

My entrepreneurial mind kicked in, and I set up a meeting with my buddies on how things were going to work from that point on. I had boxes of flyers at my house. They were going to come by each morning, pass out the flyers, and come back to my house around 11:30 am to go eat. It worked and went very well for a few weeks. I was getting my first taste of being "*the boss*" *and* loving it.

Unfortunately, it would not last. The destruction of my four-dollar-a-day empire was about to crumble.

My buddies started throwing the flyers in a dumpster behind the plaza, which was the same one Dino's Pizza used. The manager caught them in action and didn't say anything all week about it until I went to pick up my twenty dollars.

"You are fired. Don't any of you guys come back."

I was shocked because I had no clue that they had been doing that, or for how long.

Work lesson #1: If you want to be "the boss", you must put in the time and energy, and not take any shortcuts.

Back to the drawing board to find another job. As before, it was very difficult to find someone to hire me. I knew I would get turned down because of my size, and not because of my drive, dedication, or work ethic. Then it hit me! Living on Patrick Air Force Base gave me an idea. Every family needed to have their lawn mowed once a week—it was mandatory. I thought to myself,

" Why not be the guy who mowed the lawns?"

That is precisely what I became, the local lawn boy, cutting all the yards that needed to be cut. I was cutting three to four yards per week, making five dollars per cut. I made a deal with my father, though, ensuring our yard would get cut first, then the others, because I was using his lawnmower. I was cool with that because I was on to something good.

I mowed lawns until it was time to start high school. I never cared how many times I got turned down. I just really wanted to work, so I never gave up.

PART 5

Big Man on Campus

HEADING INTO HIGH SCHOOL, I was looking to make a name for myself. I was a huge fan of professional wrestling, and I knew I had a chance to make the high school varsity wrestling team. I had wrestled in the seventh grade back in Germany. Some of my closest friends in junior high had moved, so I was nervous about not having them around. I walked around the campus and saw a few old classmates from junior high, but I needed to find where I fit. I concentrated on my classes, to make sure my grades were up to par, and started my journey of making the wrestling team.

I remember going into my physical education class and meeting my coach, Ms. Judy Hedgecock. I didn't know what to expect from her. She was a very stern and no-nonsense type of person. Me, being the funny guy, didn't want to get on her bad side. She saw me working out on the weights and asked,

"Are you going to go out for the wrestling team? You would make a good 100-pound wrestler."

I smiled as she gave me a smirky look. I found out, after a few weeks had passed, that she was really taking an interest in my weightlifting. She changed my life in the weight room. I didn't realize it at the time, but under her guidance I was on my way to becoming the strongest student in our school, pound for pound, on the bench press. I took my max to a 210-pound bench press at a body weight of 93 pounds. I really admired what Ms. Hedgecock did for me as a person and athlete because she was very humble about not letting me know about her world-class softball career and coaching until later.

I was pumped up about the upcoming wrestling season, but I had three seniors in front of me shooting for that varsity position in two different weight classes, 100-pound and 107-pound. Let me remind you, I only weighed ninety-three pounds on my best day! I wasn't going to back down from this challenge. I was there to make the varsity team. We were three weeks away from the beginning of wrestling season, and the talk around the school campus was that Ronnie, a senior, had the 100-pound weight class sealed. I started to gear my mind to seal the deal in the 107-pound weight class. Two seniors, Jim and Vincent, were in my sights, and I was sure someone was about to take a back seat to me. The day finally came for the "wrestle-offs", which are drills to see who will be on varsity or junior varsity. With the strength I had gained in PE with the help of Ms. Hedgecock, I went on to win the wrestle-offs to become the only sophomore on the varsity team, everyone else on the team was a senior. As the season went on, I was getting beat a lot. Those fourteen pounds and twelve inches in height I was giving up each match was taking a toll. I was making no excuses.

I was putting up a great fight with the knowledge that the next year I would be a lot better. I ended the season with seven wins and eleven losses, but I was proud to have made the varsity team. I promised myself that the following year I wouldn't get pinned again. That was the worst feeling. My head was held up high, knowing that against the odds, I achieved my goal in making the varsity wrestling team, and benching my max of 225 pounds by the end of the school year. I saw greatness coming in the near future. My first year of high school showed people that my size did not stop me from doing anything I set my mind to.

**Always believe in yourself and push
to be the best version of yourself.**

PART 6

The Mat

My parents had a new house built during the latter part of my sophomore year. I was on the move again, and ending my final two years of high school, in my seventh school. Being short with dwarfism didn't make things easy when you're the new guy. I had set my mind to achieving my goals by being one of the best wrestlers at my new school, Palm Bay High. Unexpectedly, I was at McDonald's, getting something to eat, when I was approached by this older man, about five feet four inches in height.

"Do you wrestle?" he asked.

"Yes," I replied.

"I went to Satellite High and wrestled," he said. "I'm Bill Stewart, the head coach of the wrestling team at Palm Bay."

I smiled. "I just moved to town."

"I want you to be my 100-pounder."

"Without a doubt!" I could barely contain my excitement.

The summer went quickly. I ended up meeting my new best friends, Mike Archer and Al Booth. We spent time hanging out and going to the mall. They showed me the area and introduced me to fellow Palm Bay High classmates. We started school, and I knew I was going to receive a lot of stares walking in the hallways in this huge high school. Nine hundred students walked those halls daily, and many seemed quite intimidating as oversized students looking like grown-ups. I arrived at my PE class, hoping I could make up some ground on meeting new friends, and fitting in as the new student. I walked over to a crowd of football players bench-pressing and yelling about who was the strongest. As I watched, one of the players said, "Somebody step up!"

In my heart I knew if I did this, it could make or break my chances of gaining some new friends. I walked up, and they started looking at me like I was crazy. The weight was 225 pounds on the bench, and I asked for a spot. Bam! Bam! Just like that I pushed up the 225 pounds, and the weight room went crazy! It was the making of *me*! Chris Hollyfield. It spread quickly through the hallways that I was a strong little dude with a smile. It made me feel good. I set my mark in my new school.

Our wrestling tryouts were coming up, and everyone knew I had my eyes on being the best one hundred-pounder to step foot on the mat at Palm Bay High. It was my junior year, and we had a young team. Four guys on the team were pushing our way into being the captains on the team. I ended up becoming one of the team captains, along with another junior, Brad Stewart. Yes, you guessed it—he was coach Stewart's son. Tyrone Dixon, 178 pounds, Tim Monroe, 134 pounds, Brad Stewart, 157 pounds, and Chris Hollyfield, 100 pounds, formed the Four Horsemen. We challenged one another to be the best, and boy, did you see some good matches!

I went on and had a decent year, with a 17–8 record, giving up no back points, and nabbing two eight-second pins. That year was a lot better for me than my sophomore year, when I had a 7–11 record. In my junior year, I was stronger and wrestled in my real weight class, at 100 pounds and not 107. I had also only weighed 93 pounds the year before. Unfortunately, the year ended without me making it to the state tournament. But all in all, I had a good year making new friends and doing well in wrestling. It took the rest of the school year to get stronger and better for my senior year, setting my sights on winning the state tournament. I started to gain interest in professional wrestling after I saw a few people on TV my size, with dwarfism, doing it. I made it clear to friends and family that I was going to make it to the next level in wrestling—professional wrestling. I trained hard, not just for my senior year, but also for the possibility of what lay beyond.

My senior year came, and I was no longer the strange little guy walking around the campus. By this point, everyone was expecting the Four Horsemen (though there were only three of us now, because Tim had graduated the previous year) to be the best. Brad, Tyrone, and I were the only seniors coming back, and our mission was to be the best. I was so pumped that year about being ranked as one of the top wrestlers in our county, and about setting my sights on going to the state tournament.

I was having an incredible year as we headed into tournament time, with a record of 13–0 in the regular season! All I could see was a perfect record ahead of me, leading me on. Then, I lost at the Cape Coast Conference to Richard Jones by two points! I had beaten him my junior year, and yet we met again in two more tournaments, and I lost to him twice more. I was heading into the state tournament with a 20–3 record. I had reached that goal, it was a matter of winning it. I got to State and won my first match! I worked hard and knew I deserved to be there. I then lost, by three points, to the guy who wound up winning the state tournament. I always wondered, "If I had just beaten him, would I have been a state champion?"

With my high school wrestling career over, I had to set my sights on other things.

Stay focused.

I was closing in on graduating from Palm Bay High School, and my wrestling coach told me that another wrestling coach, from Rockledge High, wanted me to come to an event at his school. They were hosting professional wrestling matches. Not knowing the reason why, I drove down with Mike West, one of my best friends. Once I got to the Rockledge High gym, coach Rich Guerra took me into the locker room to introduce me to Don Miller, the southeast regional promoter for Florida Championship Wrestling, and new wrestler, Lex Luger (who would later be known as the "Total Package"). Don and I were speaking about me getting into pro wrestling, he gave me the name of the person who could train me— Lord Littlebrook, out of Saint Joseph, Missouri. If I wanted to be the next little person professional wrestler, I was going to have to decide between community college and professional wrestling. Looking to fulfill my dreams, I felt so much pressure, and I knew I would have to get my parents blessing.

Using the half nelson on my opponent.

The summer was coming to an end. I was still fighting within myself to make a decision to attend the local community college, and make my parents happy, or go to Saint Joseph, Missouri, and start training to be a professional wrestler. I didn't want to leave friends, family, or my high school sweetheart, Tonya, or the job I had on Patrick Air Force Base. I made up my mind that I would at least take a semester at Brevard Community College to see where my heart was. As time went by, I was in the gym training and doing my studies at BCC. While attending there, I was still around a couple of my closest friends, Mike West and Delmar Richardson, and I would tell them I had spoken to Lord Littlebrook, and he was patiently waiting for me to come and start training. As we sat down one day during our lunch, our progress reports had come out, and my grades were barely passing. I knew then that at the end of the semester I would be gone. All I had to do was tell my parents that it was official. This was not going to be easy. I waited a few days to tell my parents, not about my semester grades, but about the fact that I had been speaking to Littlebrook. I wanted to head to Missouri and start training to see my dreams come true. I left in March 1987, leaving everything and everybody back in Florida, because I was determined to be a pro-wrestler. I landed on a Friday night at Kansas City International Airport and was waiting on my ride: Little Karate Kid from the World Wrestling Federation. He was to pick me up and take me to my new home for the next few months or years. On the ride back to Saint Joseph, Little Karate Kid, known as Kato, gave me pointers about what to do and not to do as a rookie in training. The next morning, we jumped right into training. I was looking at six other little-guy wrestlers, including Little Mr.T and Little Cowboy. It was show time. Coming off a great senior year in high school wrestling, I was ready, even though there was a big difference between the two.

I was pumped, and it turned out to be a good first day. Within a month, only four short weeks, I was heading to St. Louis to wrestle in my first pro- wrestling match. My first wrestling name was Little Tiger. The wrestling match was not for the WWF, so I had no idea what to expect. I drove three hundred miles in a small pickup truck with a fellow wrestler by the name of Bad Boy Brown to get a taste of my dreams becoming reality, and a glimpse of what was to come. Pulling up to the building, which appeared to be a run-down bingo hall, I was in shock. I had no clue that my dreams to wrestle on TV, in front of thousands of people, was going to start off like this.

I told myself, "Chris, you've got to start somewhere. Here we go. Let's do it and do it good."

It turned out to be a great match, with one hundred people in attendance. I was a pro- wrestler, baby, not knowing for how long. For the next week, Bad Boy Brown and I would travel all over Missouri, battling each other as we shared this journey together. Finally, ending back at Saint Joseph, Missouri, the promoters gave Lord Littlebrook a good report on me, so I was hoping for the blessing from him to let me wrestle in the WWF. Weeks went by, and I was still doing the small shows and lots of highway driving, and I asked Lord Littlebrook at dinner one night when I could move up. Boy, did I find out the hard way that, as a rookie, it wasn't good to ask such questions, (or any questions, for that matter), because it got heated! I'm a competitor, and I felt I was ready to shine. I didn't know it was going to cause major problems.

He told me during a training session that if I didn't like it, I could leave right then. I had a lump in my throat, realizing this was something serious. Here I was, fourteen hundred miles away from home, at the tender age of nineteen, not knowing what to do next. I decided to leave and stayed with Bad Boy Brown for a few weeks until I flew back to Palm Bay, Florida. My parents were happy that I had come back home, as were my friends and high school sweetheart. When I left Saint Joseph, I knew that my pro- wrestling career wasn't over. I just didn't know where my next opportunity would come from. Once I got back home, I was planning on getting back into college somewhere.

One night in 1989, hanging out on the couch in my apartment in Tampa, Florida, with my college roommate, I was flipping through the channels on the TV. I came across a commercial for a Florida championship match that was being filmed just down the street. Not knowing if it was fate or coincidence, I decided to head down to the television studio and see if I could get in. I really wanted to be seen. To my surprise, I was allowed full access. I was soon talking with the famous wrestlers, Steve Keirn and Kevin Sullivan. Kevin had the idea of getting me to team up with himself and a female wrestler named Luna. I agreed, and it seemed, just like that, I was back in the saddle. But, after a couple of matches, the partnership fizzled, and I was back to square one.

PART 7

Dreams come True

IN 2007, I WAS SITTING at my business office at the time when I got the phone call that knocked me off my feet. It was the WWE calling!

"Is this Chris Hollyfield?"

"Yes."

"Would you be interested in wrestling as Little Boogeyman with Boogeyman?"

First thing out of my mouth was, "Yes!" Then I thought for a quick second. "Are you guys joking with me?"

"No," he said.

I didn't believe it was real. "Can I call you back?" I called back after I had gathered my thoughts.

In a serious voice the person on the line said, "Are you ready now?"

I was still in shock. It was really the WWE talent office! A representative had finally called me after twenty years of chasing this dream. The representative told me to go online to see who they were talking about. At this time in my life, I was forty years old, and I wasn't thinking about wrestling or WWE. That was because of the experiences I had in the past in the wrestling world. Let's say this—I had gotten burned a lot, and it had left me with a more negative view. At the same time, I was thinking,

"It's my time to shine."

With a smile still on my face throughout the conversation, I suddenly remembered something that I would have to consider before making any decisions. I had recently opened One Haven Home. It was a group home for at-risk teens. This was a twenty-four-hour business, nonstop, no holidays. I had a big decision to make. I met with my parents, who were also my business partners, and asked them if they could cover the days I was gone. They said they would, and that gave me the green light to continue to pursue this dream and head off to WWE. A week later I was on a plane to Seattle, Washington.

I got to my hotel, walked to the elevator, it opened slowly, and—Holy Moly! This six-foot-four-inch man reached out his hand and said,

"Chris Hollyfield, thank you for being a part of this." It was Vince McMahon!

As we took the elevator, he was talking about how slow it was, and I was standing there thinking, "No way. I'm here at WWE." It was an amazing feeling; chasing your dreams for years, and finally realizing they were coming true. We both went to the weight room, and as I finished up there, I went over to him and said, "Thank you, sir."

I ran back to my room, wanting to call my friends and family. My life was on a roller coaster. In this business, I never knew when it would end, but I was ready for the journey regardless, and I was going to show the world who I was.

I got dressed. Call time was 11 am, and I didn't want to be late. I drove over and watched as fans stood outside, waiting to catch a glimpse of the WWE stars, not knowing I was next on deck. As I parked my rental car, I saw other WWE stars giving me love, saying, "Welcome, brother." These were stars such as Booker T, Randy Orton, and others. As we walked through the tunnel, I saw everybody I had been watching on TV, and in my mind, all I kept saying to myself was, "Chris, make sure you shine and make them want you back."

I saw a sign that said WWE Locker Room. Time to put the game face on! I walked in and saw wrestlers I had watched on TV as a kid. I kept it cool. "Yes, sir. Nice to meet you."

Dusty Rhodes, the "American Dream", walked toward me and said, "Hey, Little Boogey."

I smiled. "Hey, Dusty," I responded. I extended a hand-shake.

I was looking for a place to put my stuff and looked up. Chris Benoit was next to me. Who would I see next? I went into craft services, that's the place where we ate, and more superstars were in there eating. I got myself a plate of food, but I got a small plate. I didn't want them to think I was greedy. I was still nervous, so I played it cool. After eating, I went back to the locker room, and I finally ran into Boogeyman. We shook hands, and he took me into the arena to give me a few pointers.
With a big smile and a few adult words mixed in, he said, "Don't mess this up."

Time passed, and 2 pm came around. It was the preshow time, so we could go over our match with Fit Finlay and Hornswoggle. It was so official. I was about to 'bring it' in front of eighteen thousand people and five million TV viewers.

Show time had arrived! It was 8 pm. I was all painted up and had a bag full of earthworms that I was to put in my mouth. I didn't know what to expect. I had never put worms in my mouth before. I was under the ring and waited for about fifteen minutes to emerge from there. Boom! Boom! I appeared, and the crowd went crazy! It was the biggest pop of the night! Yes, people, Little Boogeyman had arrived! From that moment, I knew I was ready for this ride.

We had a good match, although we lost. But afterward, I got lots of love from Vince and the other superstars. I took a walk to the bathroom for privacy to celebrate. This journey took me for one heck of a ride, and there were ups and downs, but I never gave up. For the next eighteen months, my life became complete with a painted face, worms, and travel all over the country.

We were finally headed to the Staples Center in Los Angeles, California, home of the NBA's Lakers and Clippers. We landed in Los Angeles that night, and fans were at the airport screaming, "Little Boogey! Little Boogey!" It was great to hear their excitement.

We were going to a "No Way Out" pay-per-view event. This was it! I was so pumped up and ready to shine! That night we had over twenty-four thousand people in the arena.

Anytime you get to shine in Los Angeles, you know you've made it somewhere! I was laughing out loud, that's for sure, enjoying every minute of it.

Our match started. The crowd was going crazy. Everything was turning out awesome, and then one mistake happened. I got thrown against the rope, came back, and Fit Finlay, who was to land a size-fourteen boot on my chest, instead planted it dead in my face! With my face feeling numb, I flew back three feet and wondered if any of  my teeth were knocked out (no tooth fairy here—too old). Suddenly, I was all over the social media feeds. Little Boogeyman was living on cloud nine.

My dream was coming true, and at the same time I was making a difference with our family business, One Haven Home. I was helping at-risk teens get their lives in check. Every Friday night I would sit with them, and we would watch WWE SmackDown together. They would ask me a hundred questions about wrestling. I tried to instill in their minds that if you focus on the positive, your dreams can come true. I would tell them not to be a follower or go looking for trouble. Just be yourself. Few got it; most didn't. That's because they wanted that bad-boy credit to fit in with the other kids who were always in trouble.

When we finally got to wrestle in Orlando, I got twenty tickets to bring my friends, family, and, of course, my kids from the group home to come see me live at the Amway Center. Little did I know that three months later I would be released from WWE. I was saddened, but it's business. When your storyline runs out, you're no longer needed. The WWE rollercoaster ride was over, but my life was fine as I focused on helping the eighty-three different kids from the group home. I'm glad they at least got the opportunity to see me perform live.

 Little Boogeyman

My journey to WWE wasn't an easy road. There were nights of falling asleep at rest stops, to save money for gas, to be able to showcase skills to make it to the one and only WWE. My dreams came true twenty years later, despite the fact that I left my family, girlfriend, friends, and government job, to be ultimately disappointed. Over the next few years, I would become a more positive figure, teaching the kids to always believe in themselves. My life has been a mixture of chasing my dreams and goals, achieving them, and learning some valuable lessons. But most of all, I try to help individuals turn their lives around, and I am there to see them smile.

As a kid, I thought being short was going to be a downfall. What I learned, though, is that my height does not get in the way of me living my life exactly how I want to live it. I have helped, enhanced, and enriched many lives around me.

I'm thankful and blessed to be who I am and have some awesome people in my life. Thank you for coming on this journey with me. I love you all.

*****Never Give Up******
My life has been a roller coaster, with many ups and downs, including not being accepted at various workplaces due to my size and not my ability. I believed in myself, which allowed me to overcome a lot of things. Every day is a struggle, having to prove yourself, even as an adult. But once again, never give up and *believe* in yourself. Champions never quit.

I am so proud to have mentored these two awesome soldiers,
Emanuel Campbell and Sha'brea King.

PART 8

Big Encounters

—Encounter with Shaq

I WENT TO A CONCERT with one of my employees, Big Dan Curry, who was six feet seven inches, and another good friend of mine, Delmar (known as D). We took a limo to Orlando in October 1992, and the venue was packed. We were having a blast prior to the concert and were wanting the good times to continue. I was in the lobby, and I saw Shaquille O'Neal trying to get in the door. I walked up to the doorman and said, "He's with me."

The doorman didn't know who he was. Shaq looked at me and back at his teammate, Dennis "3D" Scott, and said, "What's up, little man?"

"Chillin', Shaq," I responded, with a *big smile* on my face.

I walked away to look for Delmar and Dan in a packed concert. I spotted Delmar as I was walking toward him but didn't realize Big Dan was looking for me as well. As

I was about to approach Delmar, Dan reached out to tap me on the shoulder. In the split-second Dan reached toward me, I turned and saw Shaq grabbing Big Dan's arm. "No, no, Shaq. He's with me."

It was really cool how Shaq was looking out for me. He took me into the VIP area and wanted to talk to me, find out who I was—pretty much just get to know me a bit. At some point in our conversation, Shaq, standing at seven feet, was next to me, only four feet four inches, and he picked me up and stood me on top of the bar in the VIP section! Oh, yeah! It was The Big Fella and Little Big Man talking and having a good time. Can you imagine what we looked like standing side by side?

That's how I came to know Shaq. When I went to Orlando Magic games after that, he remembered me. Funny thing—on our ride home I was teasing Big Dan that he almost got the smackdown from Shaq! The look on Dan's face was priceless!

—Encounter with Donald Trump

On April 1, 2007, I was heading to WrestleMania 23 in Detroit, Michigan. This was WWE's biggest event of the year. I didn't have any idea who Boogeyman and Little Boogey were going to wrestle. As I arrived at Ford Stadium, home of the Detroit Lions, I received confirmation that we were going to be doing a skit with Mr. Donald Trump himself! As I left the locker room, I saw Trump walking toward me in the direction of the green room. We approached each other, shook hands, and said hello. A few hours passed, and it was time to go over our scene before we started filming. Our scene was shot backstage, so the eighty thousand fans in the stadium could see it on the "Big Screen".

As we started filming, Trump began taking charge, and it wasn't even his call or show. The scene was shot. It took longer than Trump wanted, and we only got one take. In the world of TV, you do at least three takes, just in case something doesn't look or sound right. After the first take, the production manager said we needed to do it over, and Trump was not having it. "No, I'm done. Going to my greenroom. Do your magic and make sure you get my good side." Then he left.

The production team called Vince McMahon, the Founder and CEO of WWE, and he was mad as he watched the clip. "Get Trump back here," he said. The response he received was that Trump was not coming back until it was time for the match. Because of the look on Vince's face, I felt like I was about to get fired. He was so mad about the entire situation. Nevertheless, we didn't do a retake, and the skit did make it on WrestleMania 23 in 2007.

Being a part of WWE allowed me the opportunity to meet a multitude of amazing individuals:

* John Cena
* The Rock

I had the best night ever in 2001 with WWF, working with Dwayne "The Rock" Johnson in front of twenty thousand people in Sacramento, California. He is now one of the biggest stars in Hollywood. What an honor.

* Undertaker
* Big Show
* Ric Flair
* Booker T

That's just to name a few, but I met the whole roster.

PART 9

Fatherhood

My world changed forever on July 11, 2012. That day, in Melbourne Regional Hospital, I officially became a father as my son, Zaiden Christopher, was born. With my heart pumping and racing a hundred miles per hour, I was there in the delivery room, holding my bundle of joy. I started talking to him as if he could see and understand what I was saying. This was my first child, and at the age of forty-five, I was having a different experience than most of my buddies, who had children who were teenagers in high school or were in college.

I was so excited about Zaiden that I was ready to play catch with him already and show him my wrestling skills. I knew in time that this little guy would be my mini me—but much taller as he got older. As time went by, Zaiden started to talk and walk, getting into everything. I would shake my head and smile, knowing the time had come for me to experience a different kind of journey—fatherhood. I always wanted to be there to communicate with my son. That was the most important thing to me. As he got older, no matter what, I wanted him to be able to talk to me during the good and bad times in his life, regardless of the things he might be going through.

Dropping him off at daycare was hard for me for a long time. I cried because I was so nervous about leaving him with anyone. After a month, I was doing better with dropping him off. Zaiden was getting older, and by the age of two, the other children started to notice that I was a smaller than the rest of the dads. They had no clue how this happened.

They would ask Zaiden or me sometimes, "Why is your dad so small?"

I would tell them, "This is the way God made me. But if you don't eat your vegetables you may also stay short like me." The fact that I was shorter than the rest of the dads made Zaiden the most popular kid in the daycare, because I was the same size as a lot of the children in the older classes.

Zaiden and I spend a lot of time going on trips, and his favorite place is Chuck E. Cheese. Now that Zaiden is five, he understands that his dad is short. His understanding is evident in simple ways, because when I am in the kitchen cooking, he is always asking if I need help reaching things. He will ask me to pick him up, so he can reach them for me. It was scary for me to have a child, because I never wanted my son to deal with the fact that his dad was physically different. His personality is so much like mine though, so he will do fine. He is very understanding. I'm very blessed to have Zaiden Christopher in my life.

First picture is Zaiden and I, below is picture of
Zaiden and his cousin Kayden.

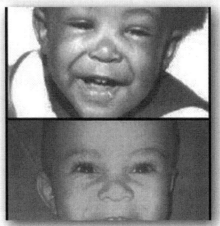

First picture on top is my three beautiful nieces (right to left Stasha,Raeven,Dionna).
Second picture is Zaiden and I, both at nine months old.

PART 10

Friends and Family

I WANT TO GIVE THE following people the biggest shout-out and love for believing in me:

God. His blessings are endless.

My parents, Ann and Lunford Hollyfield. I cannot thank you enough for your love and support.

Mr. Ivory, for helping me start my first business, Fresh Cut Lawn Service.

My grandmother, Rosie L. McCovery, for staying in my ear all this time.

Mr. Archer, for always teaching me some good old-school knowledge to learn from.

Mr. and Mrs. West, for keeping us in line.

Mr. and Mrs. Bowers, for all the sleepovers.

Mr. Love and Sandra Carter, for always making me feel like a star.

Mr. John Holder, for being a mentor and traveling with me.

Mr. Ron Gallagher and Company, for keeping my Got Respect Tour going.

My sister, Sherri, my brother, Scooter, and my nieces, Raeven, Sasha, and Dionna, for all the love.

My aunts and uncles from Cleveland, Ohio, for family is everything.

My aunts and uncles from Pensacola." Who's your celebrity?"

My aunt and cousins from Houston, Texas. Keep smiling.

My cousins in North Carolina. Stay focused.

My cousins in Detroit, Michigan. I don't give up.

My cousins in Atlanta, Georgia.

Coach Stewart. This man was one foot taller than me! Made my day

Coach Stewart

My history teacher, Mr. Brothers. All I can say is that he only had to tell me once. Thank you, sir.

Ms. Jones, who gave me my first real job after I filled out countless applications.

Mike West and family.

Mike Archer and family.

Tyrone Dixon and family.

Delmar Richardson and family.

Thank you, guys, for making me part of your families and allowing your kids to call me Uncle Chris.

Matt Todd and family.

Rob Johnson and family.

Preston Centuolo and family.

Dwayne Bowers and family.

TJAY and family.

Jon Absey and family.

Pam and *Stand4kind,* for allowing me to share the same goal and to make a difference for students and schools.

Got Respect Tour

John and LaVerne Perry, for guidance and leadership.

Ellen Little, for sharing plenty of her time. Thank you.

Fellow Palm Bay and Satellite High School classmates; you were all a part of this journey.

All the students I've seen and met over my years of touring. I thank you all.

My boys in the Under 5 Foot Club. , pictured left to right Chris Rutte, myself, and Jeff "Pitbull" Patterson.

Billy Klinke and myself out having lunch.

I truly thank you all. For we each play a part in one another's lives, and you have certainly played a crucial role in mine.

I would like to take the time to tell you about friends and family who have been with me through the various phases of my journey so far. I want to start with friends. First, let me express that these individuals cut me no slack because of my height. They didn't care about that then, and still don't care now. Whether I was right or wrong, they were always the same, providing me with support.

MIKE WEST

Let's start off with Mike West. Mike and I played baseball against each other, back in 1979, while in Germany. We were part of Baseball All Stars. His team came in from Frankfurt, Germany, about three hours from Spangdahlem Air Base in Germany. As the players arrived and got off the bus, we were each assigned a player to bring home and feed and show around, even though there was a chance we could meet up in the All-Star Championship Game. Mike was assigned to me. We walked around the town and got to know each other well, despite not knowing what was about to happen. Later that night, we had a dance contest at the youth center and wow! Mike won the dance contest! The prize was Snickers and a Coke, but the real prize was how much fun we had. The next day, the tournament began, and these two new friends ended up playing each other in the championship. After six long innings, we brought in our ace pitcher, Ronnie Rush, who had a very wicked curve ball, striking everybody out. We were rolling and feeling good as the game went on.

Crack! The Frankfurt team connected with the ball and runs started coming in! Our luck had changed, and the championship game was not turning out how we had planned. Would our new friendship be in trouble no matter who won and who lost? We lost 7–5 that game. The top two teams in this tournament would head to Belgium. The team that won there would head to Williamsport, Pennsylvania. That's what we were aiming for, the home of the Little League World Series, and there is nothing wrong with dreaming, right?

As it turned out, Mike and I met up again in Belgium for a world of fun and baseball, not knowing what to expect from the other baseball teams. Well, let me make this clear. Those teams from Holland and Italy put a beating on us! Mike's team and my team didn't even belong in the same stadium! I mean, it was ugly! The ten-run rule was applied twice! We took it all in stride and enjoyed the fact that we had made it that far and had fun doing something we loved. We walked back to the gym, played sock ball together, and slept on cots. The next morning, we were all leaving to go back home on buses. We hugged and shook hands, said our goodbyes, and wondered if we were going to see each other again.

In 1981, my dad was stationed at Patrick Air Force Base in Florida. To my surprise, Earl West, Mike's dad, was stationed there as well! School started, I was running around looking for my classes, I ended up in the stairwell fumbling around with my books, and I ran right smack into my friend from Germany, Mike West! We looked at each other and both thought, "I know you." With our wide Kool-Aid smiles, we immediately remembered the good old days. After a few days, we had finally caught up on all our goings-on from when we had last seen each other. Mike became a permanent part of my journey. It has been thirty-seven years, and Mike and I still talk daily. He lives in Gainesville, Florida, with his wife and kids. I moved to Palm Bay, FL.

Mike and I on the left side, and the two of us with his son, Mike Jr on the right.

MIKE ARCHER

I was riding my Honda 50 minibike through the neighborhood and came across this thirteen-year-old kid by the name of Mike Archer. He had glasses, and a big Kool-Aid smile on his face, and was waving me down. He was outside with his brother and sister doing yard work. I eventually stopped, and we started talking. Shortly after, I was picking Mike up for school. He was two grades below me. Mike would catch rides with me after school, because we both stayed for practice, since we played high school sports. He was on the baseball and basketball teams. Our friendship grew, and Mike would come visit me when I was attending college in Tampa, Florida, until he went into the military. He joined the Marines, and for the next four years he would call me during his free hours to tell me how he was doing over in Japan. Mike finally got out of the military and moved back to Palm Bay. At the time, I was living in Saint Thomas, Virgin Islands. Once again, our friendship was separated by distance, but that didn't break the bond we had created. After Hurricane Maryland hit the Virgin Islands, I moved back to Palm Bay, and went back to rolling with my dude Mike Lowrey—oops—Mike Archer (inside joke). This guy and I have had many, many laughs together, and to this day, Mike, his wife, Paula, Mike Jr., who is my godson, and Lacy are still in my life after thirty-three years.

TYRONE DIXON

Tyrone Dixon was on the football team when I met him. He pushed me hard, since 1984, and I must say, he hasn't let up to this day. Tyrone and I have been around creating memories, stories, and lots of laughs for quite some time. We met in the weight room when the football team was working out, and Tyrone was one of the strongest guys in the school, if not The strongest.

They were warming up with 250 pounds on the bench-press. As I watched, he said,
" Come get some if you can."
     I knew I had at least two to three reps in me. I walked over, and he spotted me as he said, "Man, lift your arms up."
     I knew this guy wasn't going to let me use the "I'm short" card as an excuse. I got on the bench and did 250 pounds five times, and walked away with a smile on my face, as in, "Yeah, now what!"
     I got Tyrone to come out for the wrestling team, and really did not know what I was getting myself into. We would be in practice, and we would all pair up with people

near our weight class, but no, Tyrone would always say, "I want to wrestle Chris." We would start the match and he would counter, "Are you scared?" Having him call me out made me go toe to toe with him. Each time, the end result was the same. He would pin me, but I always put up a fight. Tyrone was our 167-pound wrestler, and I was only the 100-pound wrestler. We wrestled together and went to the state tournament our senior year, 1986. We also went to prom with our dates, and all those experiences led to the friendship we have today, and have had for over thirty-two years.

MATT DREW TODD

As I became popular from TV and wrestling, I had a guy approach me by the name of Matt Drew Todd (yes, three first names). He was working at Chili's, going to school for criminal justice, and had a wife and three boys. I met with Matt for lunch one day, not realizing we had spoken years ago. As we ate lunch, he told me he wanted to be my personal bodyguard. As I was listening, I was thinking to myself, "This guy really thinks I'm a star." I'm cracking up on the inside, really digging this guy. I'm about to have my own bodyguard. For what? I don't know, but it sounds cool with me.

Matt and I started communicating on a regular basis.

I got a call from a TV producer. He wanted to do a reality show about me as a private investigator. I called Matt and asked him to find a company that would allow us to intern with them. Matt found a company, Catch & Detect. For a few years, I was doing PI work, whenever my schedule would permit. Matt and I got to travel all over the state of Florida, doing overnight stakeouts, and sleeping in cars, just to catch our subject. That was a wild ride! It was exciting, yet at times very boring, until Matt fell asleep (Yes, I am a prankster with many good stories to tell). As I got busy on my speaking tour, Matt got his bounty hunters license. Time passed, and Matt and I are still good, going on twenty years. His boys call me Uncle Chris.

Delmar Richardson

I have had many great experiences and friends, but this particular friendship is interesting. I came in contact with Delmar Richardson my senior year, when I was dating his sister Tonya. She was my high school sweetheart, and he was her older brother. We were OK friends at the time, but not super close because, well, let's face it, who wants his best friend dating his baby sister? Nobody does. Delmar and I went to Palm Bay High and Brevard Community College. While in college, our friendship grew when Mike West, Delmar, a few other guys, and I pledged a fraternity. Remember, we were at a community college, and you were supposed to wait until you were at a university to do this. We jumped the broom, and, boy, did we almost get into trouble with that! That incident brought Delmar and me closer because, from that point on, to this day, Delmar and l laugh about the "what ifs" of our early college years. After some time, his sister and I broke up. I moved to Tampa to finish up college, and Delmar came over shortly after to get his degree. Delmar and I are still best friends. We go fishing a lot now, and we are waiting to catch that big one that keeps getting away! Delmar and I have invested thirty-three years in our friendship.

JEFF "PIT-BULL" PATTERSON

I heard about this beast, Jeff "Pit Bull" Patterson, standing at four feet nine inches. He reminded me of the great pro-wrestler Paul Orndorff Jr., a former WWE Hall of Famer. Jeff was built just like him except, a miniature- sized version, and lots of attitude. Years passed, and I finally met Jeff in Chicago at a TV taping of a very popular talk show hosted by Mr. Jerry Springer. He invited us to play security personnel on his show. There were other little-guy wrestlers trying to position themselves to get that fifteen minutes of fame. During that fourteen-hour day, Jeff and I finally got that chance to get to know each other better, after years of hearing about each other. Jeff, at the time, was living in Arizona, and I was living in Florida. We knew this was time to bond and build on our newfound friendship. Since that time, we have met all over the country, having wrestling matches together, as well as against each other. Can you imagine two little guys like us going at it in the ring? Title this match Mr. Personality (Chris) versus Mr. Attitude (Jeff). At times we would butt heads, but at the end of the day, it was all a show to entertain thousands of people from all walks of life. To this day, Jeff and I have remained friends for over eighteen years. As Jeff would say to the rookie wrestlers, "I'm 'Pit Bull' and that's 'Real Deal' Hollyfield. We do legend matches."

CHRIS RUTTE
Chris Rutte is one of my buddies in the "Under Five Foot Club". He is a Canadian I met back in 2000 in Picton, Ontario, a small town one hundred miles east of Toronto. We met during the tryouts for the Canadian Half Pints, a basketball team that was made up of little people with dwarfism. They were a shorter version of the Harlem Globetrotters. We made the team, and traveled all of Canada on tour, spreading the positive message to not bully others. Chris and I connected fast because we both had the same name.

One day he turned to me and said, "Hey Chris, call me whole wheat."

For the next ten months, we went from strangers to the best of friends. In 2005, I was invited to play a basketball game against an all-boys prep school in Miami Beach, Florida, and I reached out to Chris (Whole Wheat), Jeff (Pit Bull), Billy (The Colonel), and our tallest player, Mike (Big Mike). We went down and showed Trinity Prep that size didn't matter on that day. We all remain best of friends.

BILL KLINKE
Billy Klinke, my best bud, was a guy I met back in 1996. Since I was one inch taller, I felt like a true boss (just

joking). This guy is my forever brother, and he was from the night we met. It was so funny. He was with his brother- in-law, who was standing six feet seven inches. I was walking into a restaurant, and they were coming out. We both had smiles on our faces. Like, wow, we are the same size, almost just an inch difference between us, and we knew that we were meant to meet. Smiles and high fives—well, low fives—and hugs began our friendship, which has lasted over twenty-two years of love and brotherhood. Billy and I had the opportunity to change lives together with the 3D Team Foundation, but unfortunate past injuries prevented Billy from traveling. For those who don't know, Billy Klinke, was the world's smallest horse jockey, and won over one thousand races. With all those victories, Billy got bullied in the stalls by other racers who said that his size was the only reason he won. Billy always said that it's not the size of the jockey, but the positive attitude in believing in yourself. Boys and girls, ladies and gentlemen, my buddy Billy and I still stand as best of friends for life.

PART 11

Swag/Stars/Journey

Me in action: smiling because I'm changing lives.

I HAVE TRAVELED OVER FOUR hundred thousand miles and hugged/high-fived over three hundred thousand students during my Got Respect Tour. I have been to over half of the fifty states and to Canada speaking to students. While on this tour, I had the opportunity to work with two NBA teams: The Utah Jazz (Jazz Bear is the official mascot), and the Orlando Magic (Stuff the Magic Dragon is the official mascot); and one NFL team: The

Minnesota Vikings (which had Ragnar the Viking as its mascot until 2015).

The Hummer H3 all wrapped up.

The Got Respect Tour is going into its seventeenth year. This been my hardest fight in life, due to the fact that people put up roadblocks for those who want to help save and change lives. I promised myself that I wouldn't let anything stop me.

Well, my life is not all about me. It's about making change for our youth. Here, during Christmas of 2015, I took twenty students, and changed their behavior by 88 percent from the year before. No magic—just passion and dedication.

I have enjoyed working with the Utah Jazz mascot, Jazz Bear, one of the best mascots in the world. Being able to change lives together has been a journey to remember.

I set a world record for the WNPF, World Natural Powerlifting Federation. In 1992, in Lancaster, Pennsylvania, I weighed in at a competition at 110 pounds. I bench-pressed 330 pounds—three times my body weight! Most athletes can only bench-press two times their body weight. No steroids! Nothing but the three Ds were able to help me bench-press that much: dedication, determination, and desire.

I have been in three movies: *Gamers, Five Days in the A,* and *The Film Festival.* I have been in a few rap videos, including a Christian rap video. I starred in two reality shows: *Hell Date,* a dating show on BET, and *Bull Run,* a cross-country racing show on the Speed Channel.

I wrestled for over twenty years with the following organizations: Florida Championship Wrestling, Total Impact Action Wrestling, the World Wrestling Federation, and World Wrestling Entertainment. During those twenty years, I wrestled as Chris Gorilla, Little Tiger, Little Booker T, and last, but not least, was world famous as Little Boogeyman. Yes, the worms were real.

I was told I would never play basketball. I was too short. I played basketball as a young teenager for the Community League. I also was on a paid contract, and traveled all of Canada, touring with the Canadian Half Pints for ten months in 2000. So much for the nonbelievers saying I was too short.

To all the students across the country: believe in yourself and never give up. The journey isn't easy, but the glory is well worth it.

When I was a senior in high school, I got a part-time job as a driver for Domino's Pizza, which made me the first dwarf driver the company ever hired! This was in Palm Bay, Florida, in 1986. My tips were to the moon and back.

Now, because of all my travels, hard work, and dedication, I have met quite a number of people. Here are some you may have heard of:

Sports:
Shaquille O'Neal—NBA
Randy Moss—NFL
Kevin Garnett—NBA
Muggsy Bogues—NBA
Kobe Bryant—NBA
Dennis "3D" Scott—NBA
Nick Anderson—NBA
Jason "White Chocolate" Williams—NBA
Doc Rivers—NBA player and coach
Kevin McHale—NBA player and coach
Orlando Magic players—NBA
Utah Jazz players—NBA
Minnesota Vikings players—NFL
Vince Carter—NBA
Tracy McGrady—NBA

Paul Pierce—NBA
Dwight Gooden—MLB
Barry Bonds—MLB
John Cena—wrestler
The Rock—wrestler
The Undertaker—wrestler
Big Show—wrestler
Ric Flair—wrestler
Booker T—wrestler
Dennis Rodman—NBA

NBA Hall of Famer Dennis Rodman and I.

Celebrities:
Jamie Foxx—actor. I hosted an after-party for Jamie Foxx at my club *The Raeve* in 1993.

Sinbad—comedian. I hosted an after-party for Sinbad that same year, 1993.

John Weatherspoon—comedian

Flavor Flav—rapper/reality star

Ludacris—rapper/actor

Trench—rapper from Naughty by Nature. He called me Shorty by Nature.

Run DMC—rap group

DMX—rapper. I actually worked with DMX, as mini DMX.

The LOX—rap group

Dave Chappelle—comedian

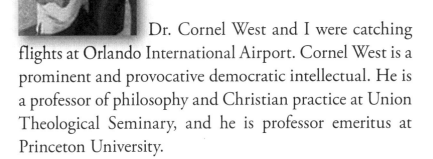 Dr. Cornel West and I were catching flights at Orlando International Airport. Cornel West is a prominent and provocative democratic intellectual. He is a professor of philosophy and Christian practice at Union Theological Seminary, and he is professor emeritus at Princeton University.

At one of my buddy's charity events, I got a chance to catch up with my friend Barry Wagner, the all-time best arena football player ever, along with one of my funny friends, comedian Joe Torry.

Red carpet BET Hip Hop Awards

After starring on a prank dating show on BET, I became the local guy from Palm Bay, Florida, rubbing elbows with stars of Hollywood, as I walked the red carpet that night in Atlanta. I ran into LL Cool J and 50 Cent. It was just the beginning to an awesome weekend.

With Kevin McHale—former NBA basketball player for the Boston Celtics in the 1980s.

Rubbing elbows with Stedman, Oprah Winfrey's significant other.

Lunch meeting with a few friends and two-time heavy-weight champion Riddick "Big Daddy" Bowe. Man, that guy can eat.

Made in the USA
Middletown, DE
08 April 2024